Incomplete Patience

Only Made Me Stronger

By Jennifer J Bowers

Copyright © 2004 by Jennifer Bowers

ISBN 0-7414-2118-6

Illustration by: Davin Williams

Published by:

INFINITY
PUBLISHING.COM

1094 New DeHaven Street, Suite 100
West Conshohocken, PA 19428-2713
Info@buybooksontheweb.com
www.buybooksontheweb.com
Toll-free (877) BUY BOOK
Local Phone (610) 941-9999
Fax (610) 941-9959

Printed in the United States of America
Printed on Recycled Paper
Published September 2004

Dedicated

To Jesus
The lover of my soul

&

To Elouise Williams
The Mother of my life

Forward

Many parents attempt to protect their children along with expecting them to play an important role in society. My poems are my children inside of my heart...every last one of them. I have nurtured them and made sure they were ready to take on the world. I have had plenty of opportunities to release them and allow them to venture out, but like any other parent, I was a bit apprehensive in letting them go. I did not want them to be rejected by society or hurt by those who handled them.

People wanted to meet, baby sit, and even adopt my children as their own, and it was not until a year ago that I began opening my heart and releasing my children to their prospects. They have loved, hated, cried, smiled, dreamed, wished, motivated, and inspired those who chose to admire them. I now know that they will survive in the world we live. I feel as though I have held on long enough and must allow them the chance to make a difference in the lives of others. All I ask is that one embrace every child and learn their real potential

My heart is my reality. If it is not from the heart, it is meaningless. Therefore, my heart is pieced all over these pages of courage. Everything I have been through since adolescence has been placed in this book. For those who never knew me, anticipated knowing me, or experienced my heart with me...this one is for you.

The title, Incomplete Patience Only Made Me Stronger, is something I jotted down this past summer while driving from Miami to Atlanta. The title eloquently honors my journey. At this time in my search to find my soul mate, I feel incomplete. But my search is over because the Bible says that a man who finds his wife, finds what is good. Patience is an ongoing process...something I have been struggling with for a long time. However, patience is something I learned from God's Word and His teachings on love. And everything I have been blessed with to encounter, whether it was pain and despair, constant heartbreak, or the misunderstanding of others, has not broken me, but only made me stronger. So even though I am single, ready to mingle, and incompletely patient about the situation, day by day I become a stronger woman.

I love life and the authenticity that it brings to nature and mankind and I have three suggestions for those who care to celebrate life. One, if you want happiness for a lifetime, help someone else. People will never express how much they need you, so you have to take the initiative to tell them, "I am willing to help you, friend". Two, get a grip and let go. Do yourself a favor and never hold on to things that do not belong to you, especially people. And last, but one that I find most important, if you love someone, never hesitate to let them know TODAY, for no one is promised tomorrow. They may just love you back.

FYI: I do not plan for the future, I live for the present.

Life At It's Best

Between the journey of life
The reality is your main voice.
When you finally come to the
Agreement that time will
Never fail you.
Let it be known, that your
Achievements are at their best, and what will
Make the cycle spin like the
Air that you breathe into.
The remembrance of the faith you had when you became a man
And decided to become
Conscious of the life in which the
Swelling of the heart makes you
Wonder why the ways are so true,
And why it lasts so long and intensely,
That you find it
Necessary to take heed and hold on.

All Over Again

But then I was like
What if I never love again?
Could I even dream of
Anyone but you?
When I speak to you
It's as if I were talking to an angel.
So easy and free.

But then I ask
Why not now?
Life isn't getting any easier
And I need you by my side.
Your encouragement
Is what I feed on
To know there is truly
A friend and a lover simultaneously
Seeking to find out
What life really means.

But then I say
Let me explain
My life and our differences
And why we are polarized.
To know that everything
About love occurs between you and me,
And why I walked back into your life
When I forced you out of mine.
Not even willing to be broken
Or shaken,
Taken for granted
Or fakin that I could
Manage life without you.

But then who
If not you?
There is no other
Not now, not ever
That will believe
In this thing called destiny.
It's effortless.
The passion, expressions
Wants, needs.
When you inhale
You breathe me
And get high off me.
It's me that keeps calling you
I am what you hear.

But then what would I do
If I couldn't have you?
That's not even reality.
Something that does not make sense.
Time has finally come
For a deeper love
To enhance this lonely life.

But then let's talk about you-
How is it that you found me?
Were you searching?
Are you lost?
Because you feel like a child
In a field of dreams?
I do.
Never again will I underestimate
The joy and pain
Shared with one person.
The one person
I prayed for.

But then I want to cry
Because I have
Finally seen it manifested.

But then I know
I want you for eternity
And to know that it is everlasting.
That look you had
When you conquered my love
And was struck with sanity.
I look at it
As if I've struck gold
Or a found a diamond,
Because a person like you is so rare
I want to hide you.

But then I want the world to know
That love does exist
And that you have come to me
Because I have waited.
The good thing I needed
To balance the chemistry
That led to confusion.

But then what does this all mean?
Meaning that we belong together
At this very moment
To appreciate life
And find happiness
When you appreciate
Life all over again.

A Moment

What comes to mind?
When you see
A man, woman, or child?
The look of grace
As one walks by
And their persona is so wild.
You think that the strut
Of a woman
Is, oh so enticing.
And the curves
Of her body
Keeps all the moments exciting.
And the man
With the build on one.
Who is suave and debonair.
Is the heir
To his throne
And the man who is just too rare.
Or the child
With laughter and joy
That seeks all purity.
While all through life
Is the search for
Freedom and Maturity.
But as the universe spins
And the century turns
Is the style of the millennium.
The touch of class

And the elegant grace
Is as much of a synonym.
You know what you want
When you look,
But what about the experience.
To be fulfilled
When the jazziness
Is so intense.
But then you venture out
And realize the potential
Of the style world,
While you're mixed in it
For the talented
Woman, man, boy, and girl.

I JUST WANT TO CRY

How long will I wait for a man
To embrace me with his life.
So I sit back and regret
All those times I was caused the strife.
I just want to know that I am loveable
And if I'll ever be enough
For that one person to know
That inside I'm not that rough.
I'll never learn to love again
Until he loves me first
By then, likely I should
Be down at my worst.

I just want to cry
That's all I want to do, and
I don't want to laugh
Because the pain is so true.
You ask me why so sad
And I'll tell you why I'm blue.
Cause I just want to cry
And that's all I want to do.

Lonely for another year
Because I was held captive.
Only to realize it was me
Who never really adapted.
Knowing now that I never loved
So how do I know that I want to.
But when I look into your eyes
I know it's the right thing to do.

7

You walked into my life
Without warning or caution.
And now that we're apart, my dear
I have this crazy exhaustion.
From thinking you'll be by my side
In the life that gives the answer.
But now I must cry in the present
Like the final show of a dancer.

FOREVER

What would it be like
To understand you indefinitely
To learn your forces
And give you me inevitably?
I wonder if you'll take
All that I have to give
And experience my love
For as long as we live.
Sometimes you intimidate me
But you're probably scared also
I believe I should let down my guard
And support you at your low.

I will be forever true
And forever wanting to be with you.
Forever is a sacrifice
And it's worth the person you are.
I've tried to express the thoughts
But it wasn't the right time.
But now the words are out
And still you're not yet mine.

I could see me sharing my life
Filling my heart with the hole,
And to share my love with you
Is a lifetime goal.
How do you feel
About our relationship now?
I want to provide you with everything
But I need to know how.

I have experienced your warmth
And seen your sensitive side
I will be your friend always
And someone you can confide.
As you can see
It's really all about you
And for our love
I'll be forever true.

I'm Sorry

I'm sorry that our lives are different baby boy
Sorry I can't fix your problems, now
Sorry you're experiencing pain, honey
So tell me what am I to do for you.
Sorry I left you, babe
Sorry I could not love
Sorry that you're scared now
So tell me what am I to do for you.

I know I should have stayed
But you told me not to wait
I said that one day our lives would reconnect.
And you looked at me with tears in your eyes
When I told you nothing mattered
And all I wanted was you.

Sorry that I'm gone
Sorry I was not patient
I'm sorry you felt attached to me
Sorry I took your heart
Sorry I didn't ask you to come with me
I'm sorry I can't hold you
You made me feel so safe
Safer than man has ever tried with me.

I'm sorry you're hurt
I'd do anything including being your wife
But you're still playing the field
And all I can do now is be sorry you let me go
Sorry you're struggling
Sorry you can't call me
I'm sorry I've given up on us.

I'm sorry that it had to end
But I'll pray for us together again
To see you back in my life
And to know
That time would be right
I'm sorry I was selfish
And wanted you right then
To know you were not ready
To leave what we had
I'm sorry for everything.

I'm sorry I did not stay
But you told me not to.

Incomplete

I want to hold you
And comfort you
Kiss you, and
Caress you.
I want to fall in love
With you
And have my fantasies and dreams
Manifested.
I want to sacrifice
All that I have
And be with you independently.
I want to dream with you
And laugh with you
Cry with you
And make sweet love to you.
I want to share
My world with you
And promise you everything.
I want to whisper
My thoughts to you
And share my secrets with you
I want to lie
On a bed of petals
And soak into your mind.
I want to wake up to you
And all your gentle kisses.
I want to forgive
And give to you
Love you and
Console you.
I want to walk with you
For miles at a time
And never look back.
I want to believe in you
To believe in us.
I want the patience

I want the faith
I want to escape with you
To never return.
I want to bathe you
And clothe you
Free you
And grow with you.
I want to see the stars with you
And wish upon them for us.
I want to smile with you
Be gentle
And wait for you.
I want to listen to you
And live with you
Be a vision to you
And breathe with you.
I want to look at you
And see our future together.
I want to feel you
When we sleep together
In our bed that we share.
I want to relax with you
After a day of confusion.
I want to know your thoughts
And listen to your expressions
Under the sunset
And wake up to you
At sunrise.
I want to know that you're content
And elated with life.
I want to finish your sentences
I want to be one.
I want the other half
That is missing
I want my life to be complete.

Goodbye

I find myself missing you
And every thought is of you
I've heard that if you love something
Let it go.
I never wanted to feel this.
I was only searching for pleasure.
How could I let this happen?
To be involved with someone so special.
The emotions that I have acquired
Are greater than I imagined
But in order to focus on life
I must let you go.

I always wanted you to know
That I feel for you deeply
And you're the only one.
Let it be known
That I will never
Leave what we have.

You have left
A lasting notion.
I have broken down
And let you in
As far as I could handle.
My mind says no

While my heart says wait,
Wait for you.
But as much as I want time to stand still
For both of us,
I must let you go
And walk without you,
But remain on your mind
When I said
Goodbye.

Heartache

Always thought you'd be there
Promises you made
It was all talk
But now it's all a fade.
You loved me, I loved you
Or that's what it seemed
We played and fought and cried
And to me, it was all a dream.
Did you really play me?
That's a question for you
Now look, you've lost everything
And will lose even more too.
I gave you my world
You gave me half of yours
It should have been equal
But you let your love soar.
Always wanted to help you
Why wouldn't you let me in
Never tried to hurt or lie to you
But still I didn't win.
My life will get better
Because I got mine
Someone now loves me
And his love isn't hard to find.
I still love you forever and ever
You were apart of me and always will be
Never can understand why you changed
We had it all, just you and me.

Don't forget me because I won't forget you
Those previous words, just pain
One day we'll reunite
And then our love will soon remain.
As a confidant, a counselor
I'll never let you go
I think of us dreaming
And the heartache, now you know.

Happiness

Happiness is all I want
       But where will I receive?
Happiness is all I long for,
       Since I was conceived.
Happiness is all I ask,
       For it seems so content.
Happiness is all I need
       But it was never meant.

Gone

Where do I go from here?
Who will I be?
How will I function for eternity?
I always thought I needed it
But actually I was wrong.
I always thought it would be there
Because of that sad song.
Never realizing it was too good to be true
For I was blinded in a shell
Never thought it would be lonely
You shipped me away like mail.
To forget the pain, will come easy
As long as there is no denial
And since I'm losing you
We'll never reconcile.

Definition

Love.
What is it?
An emotion?
A depression?
Seeking to find the meaning
Someone inform me please.
Does it hurt?
Is it happy?
Do I really want to know?
Maybe later, hopefully soon.
I know I'll be shown.
Maybe you've been there.
Had a bad experience.
Maybe a good one
Sensual maybe?
Sexual, um?
Is it kind?
Is it deceiving?
Who deceived you with love?
Discouraging?
Humiliating?
Why do I see it this way?
Have I been depressed?
Hurt?
Happy?
Deceived?
Discouraged?
Humiliated?
Could I have experienced the true definition?

Quest

Why are things the way they are
And can't do anything about them?
Are we ever going to overcome
The pain that pushes us back
And come forward out of darkness?
There are so many questions
In the back of the mind
And the ruling of authority
Controls the change.
Left in solitaire with anguish
To search the quest
And lose control in doing so.
Why are things so hurtful?
Can't find the answer?
Until then...don't ask for the quest.
They keep telling me I'm too young.
Why do they treat me this way?
Not sure if I'll be able to cope later.
Will I have responsibility before it's too late?
Sometimes I feel trapped because of Generation X
Instilling the corruption.
Curious about my doings?
What do I do?
So much anger to be released
But what will be the outcome?
Will it be appealing to the senses?
Or will they be surprised?
Probably not,
Since they think they know who I am.

I wonder at times
What I'm doing wrong
Why is no one happy
With my actions?
But do I really need to change?
I fell I am normal
About as normal as I'll get.
I feel like I have lost everything
Oh, and also everyone.
I don't want to be coldhearted
But I feel it rising
It's not me
It's not I
I'm not myself
Just let me be.

A good man…

…always looks you in the eye
…is sensitive and compassionate
…cries for you,
and doesn't mind affection.
…is always there for you
through thick and thin.
…shows his love in spontaneity
…never hurts you
but always heals you.
…must be the one
that lights his lady up.
…is like Romeo searching for Juliet.
…knows what he wants
and will go that extra mile to get it.
…doesn't play games
and will never ask for sex.
…will read these lines and see a reflection.
…is what I need,
because all the others are Bad, so…
A good man IS hard to find.

Gift

There are gifts of
Life
Love, and
Happiness
But one that is precious,
The gift that shouldn't
Be given away until
That love is dear.
The gift that only comes
With marriage between the
One you love.
The gift that no one can have
Unless you don't
Protect it.
The gift that comes
From God
Given to all his children.
The gift that was meant to be
Kept until that day of holy matrimony.

Senses

I feel like I'm losing my mind
I feel like an innocent child
I feel as if I will never succeed
I feel like I've struggled a mile
I know I am original
I know I am loved
I know change is difficult
I know the one above
I hate the racism
I hate the law
I hate the corruption
I hate the things I saw
I love God
I love Jesus
I love the Holy Spirit
I love my Savior.

Dear God,

Take me
Hold me
Show me the way
Let me know I matter
Take all the pain away.
I don't want to cry
I don't want to weep
I feel like it will never end,
Will it be like this forever?
I'm not supposed to fear
For I have you by my side.
Comfort me
Wipe away my tears
For there are many
Take these burdens from my heart
And soften it please.
I'm asking because I need your help
Cause I took matter into my own hands
Please, if you're listening
Make this pass.

First Encounter

You don't seem to understand
How much you put over me
As I see you walk with that
Badboy physique.
Wondering if there's a soft bone somewhere.
I look into those brown eyes of yours
And I see someone who would make me happy
And someone who could make you happy.
I feel like we could be together
But there is some type of static
All I want is to be held in your embrace
And I know the pain will be alleviated.
I know you're the one
By the way our eyes capture the moment
And I hope there could be many moments
Looking into those oceans wanting to jump in
Wondering if you'd rescue me
From the pain I feel for you.
I know you're what I need
So let me know what you need.
Oh, by the way…
I care about you.

Candlelight (understanding)

I sit in candlelight
Looking at your photograph
I remember when you cared
And the good times we shared.
In my diary I'm reminded
Of your presence
But now all I have are memories
That I can't put to rest.
In this illumination
I see my laughter that you seemed to enjoy
I remember the late night calls
And the things I did behind the walls.
I sit in understanding
Because I'm still enthused.
But from my understanding
The candlelight really means:
The **Brightness** I had when you called my name
The **Gleam** of your softness upon my hand
The **Knowledge** I had when I chose you
The **Fire** you showed me when I released my emotions
The **Burning** I felt when I kissed your lips
The **Dawn** we stayed up in each other's arms
The **Shine** I saw when I looked at you
And the **Understanding** I have to let it all go.

DESTINY

It has been days, months, and years
That brought us to our destiny
But I don't want to wait
For another chance with you.
You have given me the freedom
To breathe once again,
And the security
To know that I am human.
I could never walk away
And believe that you would still be standing there.
       The structure of the brightest star
       And the coolness of the wind
       Has showed me
       That all things are possible.
       I have been restored
       Due to your involvement
       And to be destined to be with you is the
              Desire I have to make you apart of my life
              Even through the unconscious effort
              Of my search to find you
              And take with me to understand all
              Insecurities about this life
              And never question the love I have for you.
              Willing to appreciate and encourage the
              Incomprehensible connection
              Between the trials that I have encountered and
              Handed over the best opportunity to
              Revive myself within your capacity
              To be in such awe with you and wanting to go
              Nowhere, but into your life.

Wonderful

Because you are wonderful to me…
There's not a night that I fall asleep
Or a morning that I wake up
Without you on my mind.
There's not a day that goes by
That I don't hear your name.

Because you are wonderful to me…
I thank God for you
And you're all that I want.
I had the concept of love misconstrued
And only experienced it in craziness
But now I know that you are my support.

Because you are wonderful to me…
I never knew where our conversations would end
As I expressed my heart to you.
It was you who gave me the sign to love again
Anything you ask of me, I am willing to do
And I want to be all that you're looking for.

Because you are wonderful to me…
It's simple things like walking the beach
Or reading my words.
Thank you for being who you are
And nothing less
So stay strong, and always be wonderful.

Why?

Why are there so many things
That rumble around in my mind?
But the only consistent thought I have
Is you, which my heart can't find.
Why is it that when I think I cry
Trying to be cordial to you?
But the tears I shed on the pillow
Are reflections of thoughts of you.
Why am I scared to find another
Who will truly mend my heart?
When all I can yearn for is the affection from you
Knowing you're why I fell apart.
Why is it when I see you
I want to feel your touch?
But I know there will be another day
So I'll long for it as such.
Why is it that I can't end it here
As I have told myself before?
But all I see is you in my life
And the only man I now adore.
Why is it that we will always be companions
But never lovers in the night?
I think I will always love you
So is that really my plight?
Why is it that I continue this emptiness
And wait for you my dear?
But it is him that I need now
And only his words that I hear.

Confused

What is it like when no one is there?
When you're invisible to the world.
Where do you fit in?
When all the spaces are full.
How do you acknowledge the truth?
When you hear it all the time.
How do you express yourself?
When there's nothing else left.
How do you maintain life?
When it's all you have.
Do you know what to feel?
When the pain burns.
Who do you know?
When the times are bad.
What is it when you can't stop?
When there is no understanding.
Where is the point of control?
When you just release it.

I LOVE YOU

How do I say I love you
But look at you with disgust?
Whenever I see you
My heart starts to sing
A song that turns into anger
Not of joy but of fear.
How do I say I love you
And I hate you all in a breath?
My mind holds an image
Of how we used to be.
How do I say I love you
With protection of the promises
That formulate in the mind?
Enough of the past
Where is my future
Maybe in the present
But no more for me to love.
How do I say I love you?
But where is my love?
The love from within…
I loathe you.

Open

I never thought I would touch again
However you touched me first.
You opened my mind
As well as my soul.
You opened my body
As well as my path.
In the presence of a man
With the smooth touch of satin
You opened my heart
As well as my arms
Which you never thought could happen.
Because I was so guarded
And wouldn't let you in
You opened my method
As well as my knowledge.
You made me feel whole.
You opened my hands
As well as my thoughts
That no one has yet been told.
About the experience I had
With someone who felt so right
You opened my eyes
As well as my mind
When you took your first bite.
Upon my neck
Is the first place you kissed
You opened my ears
As well as my mouth
And that was something I always missed.
For so long I waited
To feel like a woman

You opened my night
As well as my day
You opened my rose
As well as my toes
That I thought you should be.
The light of my mortality
You opened my passion
As well as my guilt
Now that I am open
What will you do?
You opened my words
As well as my skills
And now my heart is open too.

Dear

Mom,
I always prayed
That one day
We would
Never fight again
And when that day
Came to me
I knew that my life
Would begin.
You've given so much
That I could
Never return
It to you,
You are the
Greatest joy
And you will never know how much I love you.
I couldn't ask
For anything more
Because I have
It all.
You are the wind
Beneath my independence
And there is no way
I could fall.
You are always there
In my time of need
Because you love
Me so,

You never let me down
And I now understand
Why you always
Told me no.
Thank you for
Loving me
More than anything
In this world.
Some say they're
Daddy's,
But I'm
Mommy's Little Girl.

Falling
4 a broken heart

Whenever I fall
It seems like I'm left alone
I can never understand
Why I can't have someone of my own.
Whenever I fall
I get swept off my feet
I can never understand
Why it's never a good one that I meet.
Whenever I fall
It seems all too good
I can never understand
Why I'm so misunderstood.
Whenever I fall
I want it to last
I can never understand
Why it's always a different cast.
Whenever I fall
I want so hard to be the best
I can never understand
Why it always seems like a test.
Whenever I fall
I'm left with a broken respect
I can never understand
Why there is never a liberated prospect.
Whenever I fall in love
I'm always missing you
I can never understand why you won't fall too.

When I first met you

When I first met you
I never knew how I would enjoy you
I'm seeking to find more within you.
I've never wanted something so bad
So bad that you felt so good.
Good on my body
Good with my body
Good for my body.
Nobody,
Has ever made me feel the things
Wrapped in your nature
Your satisfaction
Something that I looked for
To give to you
Unconditionally loving
Only you.
To fulfill my needs
I need a good man.
When I first met you
There was nothing I wanted
Nothing from you
From within me
Is what I wanted you to see.
To see how you would react
To see if you would accept me
To accept you
You with me

With me is what I want
You to be
To be with me
To be with you
You are what I want
What I wanted
When I first met you.

When I'm with you
For my future husband

It's like being in love again
It's like a baby crying
It's like a young girl playing
It's like a sweet embrace
It's like rain falling
It's like springtime
It's like a bird chirping
It's like a rainbow
It's like the scent of a woman
It's like the birth of a child
It's like a sunny day
It's like a full moon
It's like the sweet taste of honey
That's what it's like when I'm with you.
It's like a cool summer day
It's like the breeze from the sea
It's like the courage of a man
It's like the heat from a fireplace
It's like my name when you say it
It's like the racing of a heart
It's like the smell of roses
It's like the wind underneath a bird
It's like the cool morning
It's like tears of joy
It's like the love from a mother
It's like the words of poetry
It's like the thought of heaven
That's what it's like when I'm with you.

Who Am I?

You will never understand me
Or even understand my pain
So then why are you trying?
I will never feel secure enough
To let you in
Or let you know me
Personally.
I don't want you to know me
You don't need to know who I am.
I'm not hard to understand
But why are you frustrated?
Take your time
Be patient
And that's how I'll know
If you're worthy of my feelings.
I don't want to hurt you
But I don't want to know you.
Why can't you see that ?
Leave what we have alone
There will come a time
When I will let you in
But as of now
I'm not dealing with the anger
That comes with being
With someone.
Yes I'm scared
I've picked up the pieces
Of my heart
And I'm not doing it again.
I'm sorry
That I feel this way,
No, I apologize
I will never be sorry
Because you can't have what you want.

I'm happy knowing
That I don't need you
Because I don't want
To know you
I want to know me.
I can't explain who I am
Until I know me
How can you know me?
Just let it go
You'll have what you want
I'll give in
Trust that
Trust me
Trust what we have now
Not what I'll give you later.

Our First Kiss

To say that you're sexy
Is definitely an understatement
But to look at your lips
And know they're sexy
Is overwhelming.
As I sit here with you
The lips you speak with
To use my name so freely
Could be those lips
To kiss my lips.
Kiss my lips gently
As you open them with your mouth
While I feel the warmth
Of your breath
Heat up my insides.
One more time
Place your head right here
Face up
Lips apart
Eyes closed
Taste and experience
The attraction I have for you
And savor every last drop
Of my anatomy.
I see that you like
The way the insides of my lips taste
Now support me as I release my body
From your mouth

Bring your lips close to my lips
And blow
Open my lips
And kiss me goodnight.

It's Not Easy

One day I will figure out
What I want in life
I'm not quite sure where
I want to be right now.
Why is it that I have no interests?
And nothing I want to do.
I want to express myself
But not verbally
However, in written form.
I want to write my thoughts
And let you interpret them
To know how I feel inside
And do whatever it is
To fulfill that happiness.
I want you to be there
Uttering my words
And grasping them
Wholeheartedly!

Soul mate

Quality is what I look for when I see you in my universe.
Wanting you to know who I really am.
Eager to know what sweeps me off my feet
Not knowing you could be the only one
That pleasures me
When I need to be in the arms of one
Who not only wants me for my body but also my mind and
Run game while playing with my intelligence honestly and accurately.
You are the one who can make me glow
And make me feel like a real sista'.
I often times wonder what it would be like to show you
How naughty I can be
To get you going
And find the one that touches your insides and complete and satisfy your
Needs to always be your
Soul mate.

Together Again

So now what do I do
Now that I have you here?
It has taken a lifetime
To be in your presence
But now I'm a little timid
Because I'm not sure
What you think of me now.
I suppose I've been feeling
The same feeling for sometime
But how do I get past
The same shyness I had back then.
You are fully aware of
The impression
But do I really want something physical
Or do I want to remain
With a school girl crush?
You still look as fine as you did
With those beautiful brown eyes.
The way you look at me
Puts me in a state of confusion
Not knowing whether to fall for you
Or admire the fact that we have met again.
I do speculate
That you admire my physical
And that is what I like about you,
Your admirability instead of tangibility.

However, your look is of pleasant control
That I have within myself
To continue to be in your presence
And never forget our first encounter
But treasure our meeting together again.

Bittersweet

I never thought
That you would be
A disappointment
In my life.
I looked up to you
And you let me down
While in my life.
I would always
Wait to see your face
But you never joined me
In my life.
There was a time
When I thought
About you being apart
Of my life.
But you went
Your own way
And left me to deal
With my life.
I can honestly
Say I love you
Because you were there
At the beginning of my life.
And you kept
In touch
But from afar
Being involved in my life.
Whenever you decided
To get in touch with me

I felt overwhelmed
While you stayed in my life.
And now I have no male figure
To look up to
Because you all scattered
From my life.
I just wanted to know
There was a secure man somewhere
To be involved
In my life.

ME

Jesus is who I have when I need that
Everlasting love when
No one else could possibly understand, being
Naive to the fact that someone could actually contemplate the
Instability that I once
Felt when my happiness was taken away, but now I have
Every intention in
Returning that love to God
Because He has blessed me with the
One thing that a
Woman could ask for to
Enlighten her world so
Radiantly and gave her the
Son of God

Lost in Love

Because I was always searching
For someone to care about me
I never cared for myself.
I never experienced confidence
I forgot how to smile
I forgot how to be cordial
I felt weak
I felt ashamed.
But since I put away childish ways
I have noticed my smile
I have heard my laughter
I have not shed a tear
I have been empowered
To do the things which make me happy
Instead of trying to please you.
I allowed myself to be neglected
All for your well being.
I pushed away those who really cared
And continued to be blinded by your voice.
But what was I thinking
I could have been so happy
Even though you made me sad
If I just would have loved myself
Instead of loving you unconditionally.
But now I have found the love for myself
Which has turned into
Emotional gratification
And extend my gratitude to you
For allowing me to see how important I am without you.

Joy

To be happy is such a joy.
You never realize how your day is brightened
When you smile so freely
Your life runs so smoothly
You're content with life situations.
The people that enter and exit your life
Are those people who share your joy.
You acquire friends who you never thought were worthy
And never thought would be given a title.
While sharing your life with these people
That you enjoy
Your day is put to rest
Knowing that you brightened someone else's spirit.

What is Life?

Do I really not want to be
Responsible for the ways of life?
I wish that life would come together
And take care of itself to stop
Why is it that one never gets what they want
However I have what I need
To complete this vicious life.
One never actually realizes
The sound of motion when you're steadily pulled by life
And all of a sudden
You drown in the waves to be rescued by the same life
That took you under.
So then why does life want you anyway?
What does it have to offer
A woman looking for a better place?
To make sure no one steals it.
Did you know that life really sucks?
Sucks the life right out of you
It makes you not even want to
Be involved in life anymore.

True Friend

Today is the day
When all that you have inside
Mirrors the Instincts that have been withheld
With the kindness of your heart
And the adoration in which you have
Developed to become such an enticing being
Expressing the love and courage
Of an adult who never
Needs to ask for that
Companion but
Yields her love to others.

Foolish For What

Why is it that women become trapped inside the souls of men
Or perhaps not the soul but the aura of the physical?
Do they think men will take care of them?
Or do they seek the pleasure of being loved?
How about we come out of the ignorance and into the reality of getting a grip.
Let go of the foolishness
Don't be mad because you think you're in love
You don't need to love anyone besides yourself
But you decide to desert yourself rather than deserting him.
Learn to appreciate yourself before you accept that someone else may appreciate you
Get the strength to become one with your soul mate
Walk side by side and not in his path
Allow yourself to be torn apart
To be placed together again by your own heart.
Believe that he will love you only if you love yourself
Your mind, body, and your soul.
Running back to the same situations is unnecessary
To the point of believing that you are all he has.
However, the days will get warmer with or without him.
Don't consider yourself alone at home
Consider it you time
Shed the tears you think he caused throughout the years you stayed
But don't leave the one you love
Just realize that a woman is never foolish
Just accommodating for that one brotha.

The Love of Readiness

Now is the time
When I know I am ready
Ready to love someone
And show them who I am.
I want to love with no limits
I want to love the one
Who is calming to my soul
The one who inquires my spirituality
And understands my fears.
To hold you tight
And make you safe
Would be the sweetest gift.
I know I am ready
To be held in your captivity
Feeling like I was the free spirit
I was born to be.
I have been through every pain
But I feel what you bring
I know that it will take some time
For you to be ready for me
And that's my love for your readiness.
I will never complain
When you acknowledge my readiness.
I just want one chance to prove
That I will be patient, honest, and trustworthy.
I think about you through my heart
And want to take you
And teach you what God has taught me.

I promise to be the greatest
At loving only you.
So what I have to offer is
Mainly my courage
To fall in love with you
I know I am ready.

My Expression

Do I really miss you?
Of course I do.
Anticipating our next encounter
What would it be like
To see a stranger
I already know
And to be scared
To meet you again?
> I took your presence
> For granted
> And thought
> You would remain in my life
> Until I walked out of yours.
> But as of now
> I'm missing you
> Like I've missed none other
> And wonder if someday you'll return.
>> We shared quite a lot
>> In the short time we had
>> And I wonder
>> Why my happiness
>> Was turned into sadness.
> Why do you keep
> Walking in and out of my life?
> Are you preparing
> To be the next blessing
> That God sends my way?
Have you ever felt
Like you've met the one
And believed
That they're all you needed?
Well that's how I feel for you.
>> I know there's a reason
>> Why our lives have split
>> However I know that soon
>> Our paths will cross
>> And we'll spend each day together.

You ask do I love you?
Yes I do.
Am I in love with you?
Everyday you grow within me
And closer to me
Everyday I ask God
To protect you
And speak to your heart.
Please do as He says
And open your heart

You were meant for me
It's a calming feeling
So strong and pure
So lasting and comforting.

And if you promise
To walk back into my life
As a man ready to be loved,

I promise to never let you go
To cherish our friendship
And whatever God brings upon us
The ups and downs
Sacrifices and willingness
Understand my sincerity
And know that you'll never be lost
When your heart guides you to me.

Uninspired

Confusion
Illusion
Compassion
Retraction
Frustration
Sensation
And yet,
Dissention
Libation
And not to mention,
Masturbation
Option
Rotation, rather than
Passion.
Am I capable
Readable
Liable, or
Controllable?
Do I want to be
Happy
Trustworthy
Or just plain
Savvy?
Sometimes there is the uncertainty
Of what you'll be up against
To find out, seek out
Seek out your role and if you fit it
Try and try again
The third time's a charm.
Don't be afraid
Fear is regret, while regret allows choices.
Uninspired?
Not fun anymore?
Approach your mind

And allow your thoughts to matter
As if they were a separate entity
Separated from the body.
Back up plan?
Always.
Accepting
Enhancing
But not wanting to be
Caring or daring
Never thought that
Giving would be so
Unmeaning.

I WILL

I'll cry you a river that runs deep into your veins
So that you can experience the rush I have for you
I'll make it feel like heart failure, when it runs rapid.
I encounter you not being here and the loneliness equals you.
Come and rescue me right now and tell me you love me so I can reciprocate.
Understand my desire of having
A friend who is loyal
A man who is true
A lover who is sensitive
A partner who is fair
And a husband who is enduring.
A mirage of you is what I see
Realizing I'm addicted to your spirit
Wishing that you would have me, knowing I would never betray you.
I will take care of you
I will never control you
I will love you as long as you allow me.
I do not have much time on this Earth
So that is why I'm persistent.
I'm like a kid in a candy store
I just have to have you
I can't wait for pay day
I can't wait until tomorrow
I can't wait to afford you
Your genuineness is priceless.
Ability
Stability

More or less it's tranquility
I will be fertility
Walking through the light
I will not forget
I will understand
I will cry you a river.

My letter to you

Dear Beautiful,

I was just thinking. My thoughts are so clear. My days get shorter, my being becomes wiser. I sit here and I try to think of something else. I can't concentrate on anything but you. My mind is uplifted. I feel so powerful. There is so much on my mind, but you, sweetheart, I never forget.

Are you receiving the messages that I am sending through God? I thought you had forgotten me, but your phone calls feel like a prisoner's joy on visitation. At this very moment, I feel a pain in my chest and that is the hole which identifies the emptiness.

I am writing for various reasons. One being that I miss you. Constantly I try to figure out how a person can miss someone so much and spent a spec of time with them. At some point I considered you a friend, someone I could converse with and depend on. But sometimes it feels like I have lost something so important to me. I never wanted to lose communication with you and as you can see I have tried my best to stay in contact with you.

I guess at this time I want you to know that I am always here for you. I don't know how many times I can stress that. I will always be real with you and true to you as a friend. Please don't close me out of your life.

Love and support,
Jenn

My Promise:

Who said they saw a rainbow yesterday?
I saw a rainbow yesterday too
I was promised a blessing
That day I called you.

It was hot and humid
And I was drenched with sweat
That was the only day I saw the sun
Because I had such a regret.

I witnessed the birth of my promise
And understood where I was going
I was complaining into your ears before
But the rainbow started me growing.

Full potential is what I proclaim
Since this new life I started
But my days haven't been the same
Remembering that Friday we both parted.

When I saw that rainbow
I was with my best friend
The two of you motivated me
Teaching that a heart should always lend.

I am now fulfilling my promise
In hopes to make you proud
My voice you can not hear
So I'll scream it out aloud.

Although you don't know my promise
You'll see a rainbow tomorrow
Know that God is always with you
And He will ease your sorrow.

You're Already Taken

I cannot have you
You're already taken
We have an ongoing flirt
But your desire we can not awaken.

I've already hypnotized you
When you looked into my eyes
You tried to manage a thought
While you construed an alibi.

You have such a character
That I find it pleasing
The concept inside my head
Would be incredibly deceiving.

Although I will never disrespect
The union which you created
An appeal in your mind
Has already clearly been stated.

Even when I inquire
A real man like you
I deeply want to explore
But there's nothing I can do.

Each time I observe you
I take some satisfaction along
But the pleasure between us
Would only be in the wrong.

I'm left with the pressure
Since your hands held my face
But I can not make the next step
At even a slow pace.

Now that you have become alluring
A question is surely raised
The rule is based on principle
Since I have you in a daze.

I'll continue to independently think
While you settle in my intellect
I know not to act on that conversation we had
The first day we met.

Be My Groupie

Worship the ground I strut on
Watch me like a hawk
Allow me to ignore you
Follow me everywhere
Pretending I don't recognize you.
But don't try and get rich
Off sex, lies, and scandals
I see you every place I attend.
Yeah your body is attractive
Your mind I still don't know
Trying to get noticed
In the midst of all my endeavors
Relax and take one step back
Inside my life I won't allow you to hack.
Pictures of me in frames
And any place I can occupy
Approach me if you can
Introduce yourself like a man.
I have a human side at times
Trying not to be judged
Like I've committed a crime
Since we're out
Why not buy me a drink
I would be modest
But I only do the best
Place you on the list
Of things to avoid
Excuse me if I'm too paranoid
Be my groupie.

Have A Nice Life

We do not even speak anymore
You have moved on in life
But you forgot how you got there.
Remember that bridge
That you burned?
Well, it still exists cause it is being maintained.
You do not realize what you walked away from
Or what you're walking into.
I expect that you are happy
I would not have it any other way.
I hope you have changed.
Decided to become a man.
Because at the rate you were going
You needed a serious back up plan.
I do not know who you are anymore.
I ask myself how could I have been in love with him?
I slept it off.
I am finally awake
From the long nap with rejection.
My dreams of you were torture.
Never anything worth sharing.
I put you on a pedestal
Allowed you to steal from me
As you had me stealing for you.
You made a divisible of twelve feel like misery
But I never wanted company.
Genuine I thought.
Best friend you screamed.

Unworthy in reality.
Unsuccessfully completing your maze
While participating with no rules.
It was instant pain when you disregarded my feelings.
Although God made it evident
That you would never be changed
The first time you cheated.
So to make a long story short
I hope she is ready to marry old routines
And discover simple truths,
So both of you can have a nice life.

A Wish of Mine

I wished upon a star
Today in the bright sky,
Hold on…
Stars appear at night,
But I just could not wait that long
· To wish for you with me.
I wished that one day we would join together in matrimony
And live happily ever after.
I wished for peace in your life
A wish of mine
While being changed
I wished for your greatness and love.
I had gone outside
On that beautiful country day
And began missing my angel.
I wished for your response.
I wished to spoil you.
I wished for that week back
But I thought deeply
And realized I would never know that experience if I went back.
This was my first wish upon a star
Trying to choose the brightest one
Thinking if you were out that day you would see it too.
Even though the day was bright
I wished that it would pour
Rain hailing down my face
Drowning in my tears.

I wish my wish comes true
When I least expect it.
I wish your wish meets my wish.
And when nightfall appears, we'll see our star
From wherever it is that we both are.

Ridin' Solo

I was born alone
More than likely
I will die alone.
I was never given a twin
Or even a sibling to push around
So when I ignore you
Like you don't exist
Please hold back the frown.
You see, everything I do
I do it for myself
I'm as independent as they come
And I love being by myself.
There's no one ridin' shotgun
Because I'm ridin' solo
All day in my zone
So I'll never get told no.
I'm calling the shots
Always taking names
They let me get in the game
Knowing now that I'm really insane.
But I laugh at the judgment
And take what I'm given
Looking at you in the background
Gawking cause you're amazed
By the girl who has truly blazed.
I'm not selfish
But refuse to think of others
I'm an only child remember
Who has had many lovers.

Don't get it twisted
For I always control my urges
Cause if I didn't
I'd have you so uplifted.
But anyway when you see me
And you wish you could ride
I'll open the door then slam it
Rules strictly I don't abide.
Don't think too deeply
You might hurt yourself
I'm ridin' solo baby
Think of me as your trophy
As I sit solo on your shelf.

You Gave Me a Compliment

I look in the mirror
And see the unpretty
You gave me a compliment
But I thought you were being witty.

I don't see anything spectacular
So why do you gaze
You gave me a compliment
But still I was not fazed.

I don't believe I am beautiful
But that's what you say
You gave me a compliment
But my baby didn't today.

You get mad because I don't accept
When you say I am cute
You gave me a compliment
Then I looked at you like a mute.

I'm not the model or magazine type
I am who I am
You gave me a compliment
But I didn't give a damn.

Flattered is what I should be
You are such a gentleman, honey
You gave me a compliment
And I laughed as if it were funny.

Nope, don't take compliments well
But I appreciate the effort
You gave me a compliment
But still my insides hurt.

My Destiny Is To Be Lonely

Will you please take my hand
And tell me everything will be okay
Grip it tight
So that I can not run away.
My destiny is to be lonely
But not wanting to grasp it
Separated from humanity
In the looks that are tranquil.
Finding out the devastating news:
WOMAN UNWANTED
It's the talk of the town
The headline story
DESTINED TO BE LONELY
Never a believer in the gossip column
But it's strictly non-fiction
Must stop printing!
Where's the press?
This can not be leaked
BITTER, MAD, CRAZY
Not again, another woman snatched by insecurity
Call the tipline!
Save her, rescue her!
For her destiny is to be lonely
Quarantine with virtues
Block out devastation
Scan for humiliation.

Inside of Me

When Mom told me you had been in existence
I felt overjoyed to have a brother.
She would have been so proud of you
Because you're inside of me.

There are times I wonder what you are doing
And want to meet you as if you were a celebrity.
I know you are looking down on Mom and me
Because you're inside of me.

You know my brother's that Mom never had?
I look at them and know you sent them for me.
I sit at the dinner table and set places for three
Because you're inside of me.

My attitude is as much of a male's
I protect Mom like you would
I love her as we both should
Because you're inside of me.

I know you see me cry because I feel alone without you.
But I feel you right there telling me, "Don't give up".
I want you to be happy for your lil' sister, they call Baby Girl
Because you're inside of me.

I look up to you, a big brother I never met.
Eight years before me you were announced.
You never let me down like Dad did
Because you're inside of me.

You gave me a chance to shine when God took you as His angel.
Thank you for letting me have our Mother that we share
I know she see's you everyday
Because you're inside of me.

Big brother, I love you so
And hope to see you one day
I'll have a son that resembles his uncle
Because you're inside of me.

Pretty Girl

Hey pretty girl
Where are you going?
Why is your face twisted in such form?
Disappointment is what you exhale.
Abandonment is unwantingly inhaled.
Hey pretty girl
Let me give you a hug.
Take you to see the bright lights.
Ask me to foster you, I think I will.
An honest person for you I will.
Hey pretty girl
Do those bruises hurt?
I know your strength by your voice.
Not another to walk away
For that undying smile I'll stay.
Hey pretty girl
Know that there's life.
For you're looking right at it.
Let me know what they did to you.
So I can appreciate you.
Hey pretty girl
My name is love,
And I need a home.
Keep me safe inside your arms.
You and I together, we'll never be harmed.

I Need You

I need you to love me.
I need to love myself.
I need you to hold me.
I need to get a grip.
I need you to care for me.
I need to take better care.
I need you to kiss me.
I need to kiss it good-bye.
I need you to adore me.
I need to adore myself.
I need you to touch me.
I need to get in touch.
I need you to be sensitive.
I need to be strong.

Love is what you make it

Love is what you make it…
    To be acknowledged
    To be soothed
    To be embraced
Love is what you make it…
    To be hurt
    To be betrayed
    To be lonely
Love is what you make it…
    To heal
    To sympathize
    To share
Love is what you make it…
    To be scared
    To be frustrated
    To be screwed
Love is what you make it…
    To laugh
    To smile
    To dream
Love is what you make it…
    To love yourself
    To love God
    To love your struggle

Your Friend
dedicated to Forgiveness

You were my friend
From the very beginning
And you made my world
Oh so complete.
The love we shared
Amongst each other
Seemed so strong
That the stars could somehow be reached.
I prayed to God
To send me someone
Who would always
Be my friend.
We were inseparable
For so long my dear
That I thought
My world would end.
I will never find another
To take your place
Because you're dear to my heart.
I love you
Forever and always
No matter how far
We are apart.

But Really In Awe, Naturally

To be alone with you
Would be a constant joy
You act like someone
Who would
Calm my soul.
I would not mind
Opening up to you
And getting to know
The survivor within you
As we speak softly
In the dark.
Have I fallen again
Too fast?
Or do I just
Enjoy seeing your face?
I have been broken
And waited so long
To have hope
With someone just like you.
Whenever I do get a day with you
My face lights up
Like the fire
I have within.
I never quite express
My feelings to you
But I think you know
How I tremble over you
By the way I quiver.

You are truly amazing
And I appreciate your style
Your emotions have been summoned
So can I have you
And brighten your cause
With the emotions I have for you?
Take me and do as you wish
You are in control.
Show me how much
Of a man you really are
And fall in love with me.

Thank You

You are the one who places thoughts
Inside of my mind
The happy thoughts
I need to get through the day
You are the one I look for
When I want to smile
And be in your anxious presence
To enjoy the times of life
You are the one who appreciates
My abrasiveness when no one else will
And makes sure that my joy goes unstolen
So that I can enjoy every moment
You are the one I want to thank.

You Are So Calming

Something about you
Keeps me searching.

You have already calmed my soul
And I feel like we should be one
And resist all temptation
To never want to be in love.

You have already calmed my soul
And now I am on cloud nine.
I have never felt this feeling
For another human being.
I hope that you will never
Feel the need to walk away.

You have already calmed my soul.
So allow me to do the same for you
Knowing what it is like
To be with a woman
Who wants to accept
All that you have to relinquish
And give in to my calming spirit
That only you have successfully discovered.

You, Only You

Sometimes I wonder if I'll ever see YOU again
If I'll make it another step without YOU
Weakness has finally set in without YOU
Not feeling YOU next to me.
What would YOU have said
If I asked YOU to stay?
YOU returned to me once
So does that mean YOU are mine?
Every thought of YOU keeps me going, and
I know without YOU
I'm in love with YOU
And YOU are the sweetest thing I ever imagined.
I cry because I miss YOU, but
Let love take over
I tell myself
It won't hurt this time.
Do YOU remember the beating of my heart on YOU
When YOU realized I stayed for your heart?
I'm reminded of the day I met YOU
When YOU hypnotized me
I try not to talk about YOU
So that YOU will slowly disappear from my mind
But the inspiration YOU send
Allows YOU to take over again.
At times I wonder if YOU still know me
But I know YOU could not forget love
And the love I have for YOU is very true.
I am not sure if these words will find YOU

But in case YOU were wondering…
I want YOU to remain in my life
I want to receive YOU
So let me make YOU happy, and know
It is YOU, only YOU that I want.

Contentment

Where are you now?
How have you been?
I'm worried about my angel
Who is also my precious friend.

Have you completed your challenges
Not knowing where they'll lead
I have one more challenge for you
Please help me find your heart that bleeds.

I respect you as a man
Knowing your every side
I want to see your love again
And be the woman that stands by your side.

I know this all seems sudden
But remember it's never too late
When will you ever realize
That you and I are the utmost fate?

Be realistic now and enjoy the time
Cherish the moments of your life
Notice how you resist the fortune
Of having me as your wife.

Attached completely to your manhood
Imagining all the commitment
Get with the program, brotha
So we can experience contentment.

Right now I'm asking all out for your hand
Not the least bit resentful
Will you marry me sweet love
Asking for your hand in marriage seems too simple.

True soul mates is what I guessed
Placed together on this creative Earth
Signs of compatibility
Since the day of each birth.

I know I want all of you
Even if I accept the secret past
But I will love you till the end
Just as long as we both shall last.

Your #1

Taught the patience
Influenced by your presence
Thank you in advance
For undying efforts

I've waited for my day
To believe to achieve
Stood body to body
Realizing you're not just anybody
Don't know who you are
Or even your life struggle
Give me the broken pieces
To create your hearts puzzle

You spoke like a shy child
Intrigued by my person
We met only for today
But it was not another day
It was another promise
That the Most High sent
I was presented with the request
Overly speechless during the process

Of the way you looked at me
When we locked eyes
And to my surprise
Definitely not the average guy
Subtle in demeanor
In all your handsome ways
My prayers were finally answered
All for me to be amazed.

Dertty Who?

To be or not to be.
What do you wanna be?
Can you be suave and dertty?
Making believe
You're the boy next door.
The outline of your lips
Is one of custom design
The structure of your mouth
Could only be created by the Divine.
Your creativity and imagination
Makes me want to become
A beat in your mind.
Something trying to escape
But too complex for even my kind.
The kind that wants to be a tattoo
On your skin
Knowing that I can always grip your body
In a way that can only be a sin.
Play with me like those cards
But allow them to spell...
J, for the juice I used to get you
E, for the explicit whispers you heard
N, for new adventures we'll share
N, for the naughty stories you'll tell, when I'm the only
1, attracted to this male.

Pardon me.

That was just the passion and conviction
I possess when you take over.
Secure with knowing who you are
And what you aspire to be.
Realize that I am forever safe
In knowing that you will never stray
Like a loyal companion
Named Dollar
Who is always willing to play.
I spit poetry
Cause I know it affects the brain
And when you inhale my words
You get high
And lose all control
As you hallucinate
Wishing I was there to roll
Those two **L's**
With my tongue
As you come out of my mouth
When I speak your name.

Smooth and sexy.
Confident and strong.
A regular woman who wants to understand your issues.
Invite me to your 'ville?
Let me invite you into **JENNTIME.**

Where there's no time like the right time
When I get you naked
Off that smooth white wine.
One last thought
As you soak into my mind
Imagining yourself soaking into me.
Let it be known
That when you seek, you will find
It's not hard to recognize
A voice with a smooth touch of satin
And know on the other end it is you.
It's you and Babygirl
And then I'll ask **DERTTY who?**

My Nature Poem

Write about the birds and the bees outside
Flowers and the trees on the trail behind the gazebo
Finding love and happiness is what I'm all about
Anticipating the relationship of one dream of mine
I'm ordered to struggle with my inner being
Conceptualize the sadness and aggression
For outnumbered is where I sit
I sit in silence hoping not to be bothered
With a smug look on my face
A school girl racing towards a goal
Where did my talent ever go
I hate not knowing anything from this education
It's all a memory that I've given up for peace
It hurts
Too much to memorize and realize
I hate this life
Check myself without balance
I can't do it anymore
Bouncing from inspiration to hesitation
Aiming for curiosity's answer
I've had enough of this pain
I want to die
Pavement mingles with sandals on a wet day
At the time of the runaway
A long stretch to even cry the tears
My eyes are dry
It's all a speedy setup.

Simple Dream

For the three times I kissed your lips
And the sixty-five times that hour you entered my brain
I thought it was time to up the tempo
To release you from this life called game.

So for the twenty-four times we made love
Before the seven times I called your name
It was love at first sight
But it just wasn't the same.

I saw you in a dream last night
Woke up realizing that you were mine
And I am yours for centuries to come
After we walk the trust line.

I need you in my life right now
The timing couldn't be better
I want to give my life to you
That dream was just a simple letter.

A letter of all our promises
To never walk away from love
Let's spend the next millennium together
Riding on the moon above.

Dear Woman and Man:

This is your soul mate
Keep one another out of harm
I placed you on this land
To walk arm in arm
Don't take for granted this destiny
Remember to remain as one
Loving each as your protection
So your souls will always be one.

Forgive me

Even when I'm making love to another man
I see your reflection in the visible air.
It took me by surprise you walking in
Knowing my vow was to never sin.
I can't keep you off my mind
And I apologize for the bond I broke
But I thought you needed to let me go
So I walked out of the limits.

You keep me thinking
As if I'm not being true
I want you to always know
That I'll love only you.

Forgive me for my man made ways
Remember to forget how I've changed
Knowing I am still your girl
And we've conquered most of the world.
It was getting too rough to stay true
Not always seeing you, I had no clue.
I'm asking for my sunshine again
Your heart, not his, I tried to win.

My Angel
aka Spirit Child

My angel flew from heaven
To rescue lil'ole me.
I am honored you chose me
Cared enough to rebuild and mold me.
Spirit child, follow me all through life.
Spirit child, dedicate your guardianship to me.
Can I drift away with you to the unknown?
It's got to be peaceful and full of joy.
Quiet and serene believing in you.
You're God's child, his most precious.
Blackout's envisioning your spirit.
A fallen angel requesting the physicalities.
Never again disappearing or whispering.
Spirit child, heaven is missing you.
Spirit child, I am letting go,
Others need you.
You are everything at anytime.
I'm missing you as I shed a tear you won't allow
But took for me and said smile.
What a blessing!

If I Never pt 2

If we never see the light of day does that mean it is dark
Or does it mean that we're thousands of miles apart?

If we never experience pain and what it's supposed to teach us
Then how would we know joy if our hearts were never crushed?

If we look deep into the eyes of the one whom we adore
In the next lifetime we might put forth effort even more.

If we depart the place that we are comfortable with not knowing where it leads
An anticipation of our hearts is one that nobody reads.

If we gave all that we had to be empty once again
Then we'd place our fears aside and begin life over again.

If we found that inspiration in someone we sought out
Just make sure they can count on trust and respect without a doubt.

If we feel caught up in the moment and hear inner peace
Include the happiness between you and I and never let it cease.

Talk To Me

I haven't found what I'm looking for
But I know it exits somewhere
I pray that it's ready for me
Taking me far away, anywhere.
All I'm attracted to is what I can't have
Knowing that it was never meant.
Did you know that I have given up?
They used me up without my consent.
For the first time I'm being true with myself.
I thought I knew my destiny
To find out life is lonely
And completely a catastrophe.
There are times when I think
And the thoughts become vague
Showing me time will tell
If I've found a gem like a jade.
Who knows if I'll find myself
Or even the one for me
All I'm sure about right now
Is the chemistry between my loyalty.

Let's Get Through It Together

You think its a game
Trying hard to complain
To visit with the insane
Turning you on to feel the pain.

Don't hold back the time
Just watch it unwind
Placing the pieces together to find
That I'm always on your mind.

You watch the symbols unfold
Letting you experience without being told
The voices inside become too bold
Don't stop, let it take complete control.

Call out my name from the inside
Release the tension that you seem to hide
I'll take you along to be your guide
But you look like one with too much pride.

So let me ask you a something
What would it feel like to have anything
To never want for nothing
And to know you were in the liking.

Caught In The Moment

Looks can be deceiving

But instead have true meaning.

You get caught up in the moment

And know it was time well spent.

Who knows if the foundation will stand

So someone needs to be at your every command.

Continue to remain to exist

Being grateful that you got your one wish.

Memory of Reality

You don't know what you have until it's gone
Then you wonder why it was placed there to begin with.
If it was just going to end that way
Then why was the flame even lit.
It's amazing how life works
Referring to the daily challenge
It seems like one big play ground
Too full to bring the baggage.
But who knows who'll walk in and out
Of the lives of every birth
Evaluate all situations
And be aware of all things to stay alert.
Is it the mental love making that seems to grasp
Or is it the common courtesy?
Replace such physical burden
With a sweet memory of reality.
It's a remarkable feeling like sitting on the moon
Consider the outlet of making a decision.
Cover all bases to extend the recruitment
And never accept tunnel vision.
It's like not being aware of what's in store
Not even wanting to open up the plan
But instead you hide behind the case
Refusing to take the appropriate hand.
Life moves at an awkward pace
Too slow or too fast for emotions
But once the spirit is clean
You can dock in the middle of the ocean.

The Beginning of the End

If words could be molded, I'd create you as the Most High did
Eliminating nothing besides your struggle
The man that every girl dreams about
The man that all women plan for times double.
We prepare to become satisfied
Instead you're marked as a standard
While I'm hanging in the clouds lifted by the vibration
Forming a distinct reason why you are a choice and officially mannered.
Worried that someday I won't occupy your desire
It's all too complex, adapting to new energy
So right now is the time for immediate action
It is luck or fortune or hopes or synergy.
View me and you in the arms of one another
Listening from beginning to end
Falling from the end of the beginning
Record my every action, reaction, location and patience not knowing the ending.
Gain knowledge as I unlock the most sacred area
Allow me to enhance your nature
Changing nothing of your design
I've unexpectedly discovered a connection in the matrix.
Capturing every direction you touched
Your willingness is overly blown
Can I be your achievement
Placing me on your most devoted throne.
I require and hold you responsible
For the exploration in such quality
I've revealed such an expression
Hoping to become something of equality.

You want your beginning to end
Follow me to the vision of beauty
Recognizing every style and character
But realize that it's only a true man's duty.

Love To Love You

Officially fell in love last fall
Ultimately you took my breath away
Unanimously my body and soul accepted it
Intriguingly at first glimpse.

Aimlessly I captured the locations
Fearlessly enjoyed every escapade
Refreshingly exchanged secrets
Patiently anticipated a bond.

Lately I haven't heard from you
Amazingly I pace my feet in your shoes
Hopelessly wanting to kidnap you
Daringly I'm too much for you.

Cautiously approached your expressions
Knowingly wanted you for myself
Kindly accepted your entity
Willingly let you replenish my heart.

Is It The Newness

Did you ever imagine
That special someone
Waiting to organize the life in which you lead
Not knowing that one woman
Would be so sensual
That her body language
That hasn't even captured your eye
Made you so delirious
That is was pleasurable and insane
To know there's no doubt that you found
A worthy jewel
To set aside
To never be sensationed by none other than the representation of your character
Trying so hard to impress
The realness in which one can conceive
Only to singe handedly accomplish a goal
That will never go unanswered
As long as there's never a lose of newness
To keep the circumstances alive
And energized by the occasion
On which a real woman takes control of
And finds her love
Has modified rewards of life regarding
Acceptance of beings and at
No time, never fearing.

Magnificent Significance

What's love if there is no one to receive it?
What good is it if it cannot be shared?
The thought cannot be compared
When one is alone in despair.
It always seems like the timing is off,
Fighting to turn the clock back on.
Missed the opportunity of turning it back period
Requesting to take only the right heart.
So no matter what love it is
It captures a picture of you and I.
Not knowing where they heard my thoughts
And placed them in a song.
It's like the singer looked straight though my chest
And sang my hearts lyrics
To tell you I'm in love with you.
Walking through life with you
Seems like a gift from God
I feel like someone made of pride
Who now walks with significance.

Praise
Dedicated to the Trinity

Lord, you hear all my thoughts
Know all my misconceptions
And at this time when I need you most
I wanted to thank you for all the perceptions.
I took what you gave me
I took who you gave me
Replying to all the situations
And occasionally breaking me.
It was urgent confirmation to allow me to see
That everything passed in front was for me
Like loving myself in order to be.
Dated from genetics allowed a mirror
So when she stands in front of it
I'm the only creation she knows
Canceling the thought of all regret and raising a beautiful rose.
Far eyes gazing at any point
But personality realized the irrelevance
Spoken so arrogantly by a misbeliever
Anyhow, stubbornness was given chance.
It was the driven insecurity laid upon my heart
Learning to crawl for my future
Waiting patiently for a conviction
To decide my lifelong torture.
So I praise you for the ability
To understand my inner most actions
And am blessed with new serenity
With a deeper love along with passions.

Acknowledgements

I want to thank God for my gift of expression. God, thank you so much for this lonely, yet fulfilled life that you have handed over to me.

Thank you to my "MA". I hope this allows you to understand your child. Without you, this book would have never been created. The encouragement and support from you is always acknowledged and forever appreciated.

Thank you to the one whom I said was calming to my soul-you know who you are. I will always appreciate your friendship and your honesty.

Thank you to my most recent inspiration. It took a stranger to show me what respect from a man to a woman looks and feels like. You will always be my "gangsta & my gentleman." Love Always.

Thank you to all my friends who understand and accept why I never answer the phone, and continue to call me rather than judge me, that is the loyalty that you have always shown me. I love you.